CATS ARE SMARTER THAN MEN

Cats Are Smarter Than Men
By Beverly Guhl

P
Pinnacle Books
Kensington Publishing Corp.
http://www.pinnaclebooks.com

PINNACLE BOOKS are published by

Kensington Publishing Corp.
850 Third Avenue
New York, NY 10022

First Printing: July, 1997
10 9 8 7 6 5 4 3 2

Printed in the United States of America

To Gary Brim with love and laughter . . .
Bev, Nunu and Hobie

CATS ARE SMARTER THAN MEN

They never ask if you've
gained weight.

You never have to ask
them to take a bath.

🐾

They'd never say,
"You call this dinner?"

They know better than
to argue with you.

They never ask you to wear
spike heels and a tight
sheath dress.

Their love isn't dependent on how clean the house is.

They'd never ask you to wear a padded bra.

They understand the difference
between laziness and a
beauty nap.

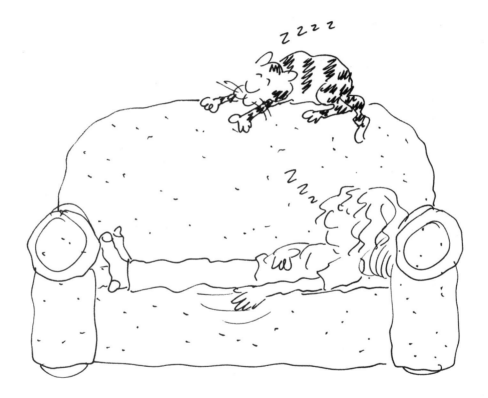

•••
😾

They'd never say, "Wear your blue skirt — it makes you look thin."

They don't drool over other women.

They'd never ask, "How much did that cost me?"

They'd never say, "You did
WHAT to the car?"

You can trust them with
your best friend.

They'd never say, "Move, honey, you're blocking the T.V.!"

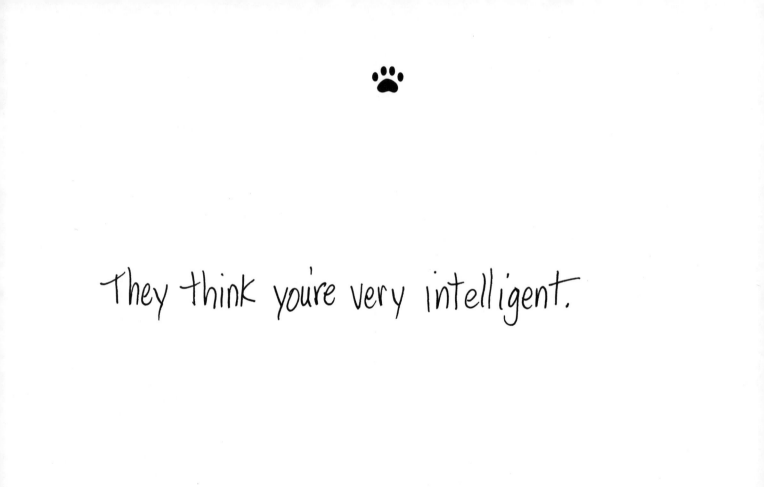

They think you're very intelligent.

They'd never ask, "So, what have you been doing all day?"

They never insist on watching T.V. while eating dinner.

They appreciate and understand the importance of affection.

They aren't aggravated by
instruction manuals.

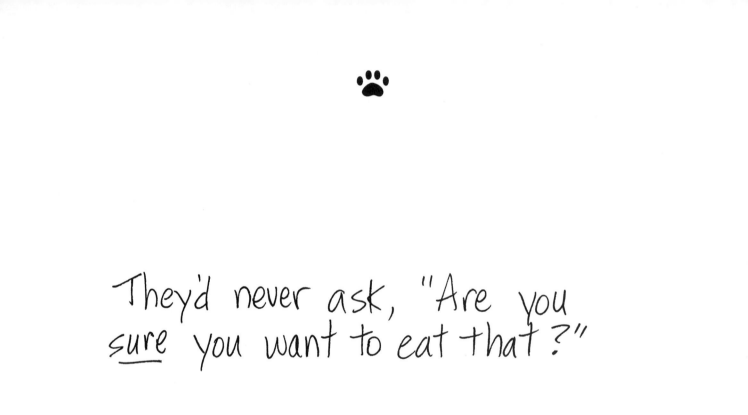

They'd never ask, "Are you sure you want to eat that?"

They don't sleep through things that go bump in the night.

They don't make you feel bad when you don't exercise.

They never accidentally call you
by an old girlfriend's name.

They would never wear white
socks with a business suit.

They know the importance of punctuality.

They would never use your toothbrush.

They don't put empty containers back in the refrigerator.

They don't run up huge
debts on charge cards.

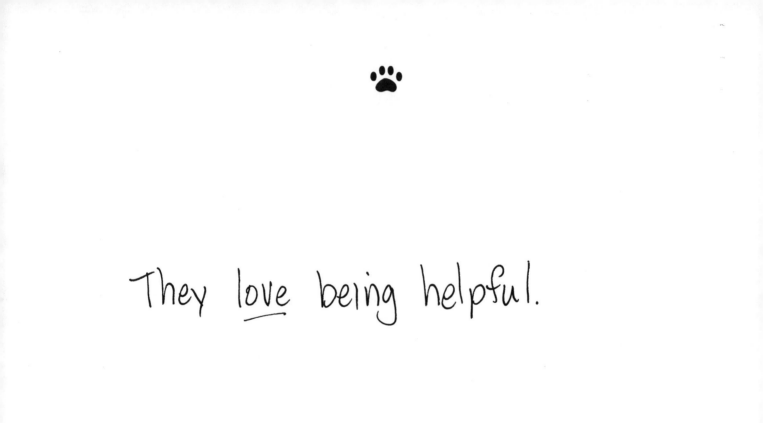

They love being helpful.

They stop using the bathroom
when it's dirty.

They'd never give you an
appliance for your birthday.

They're not dependent on
you for all their meals.

They agree with everything
you say.

They'd never say, "Why can't you look like _that_?"

They always appreciate your efforts in the kitchen.

They never question how much money you spend on phone calls.

They don't have "platonic" female friends who look like movie stars.

They don't try to
psychoanalyze you.

They never tell you what to do,
when to do it, or how to do it.

They're always sincere.

🐾

They don't try to fix
things themselves.

They never make you cry.

They don't ask you to
wear erotic lingerie.

They love it when your
thighs get fat.

🐾

They aren't interested in you only for your body.

They still love you even
when you're moody.

They don't make fun of your taste in music, television shows, books, or anything else.

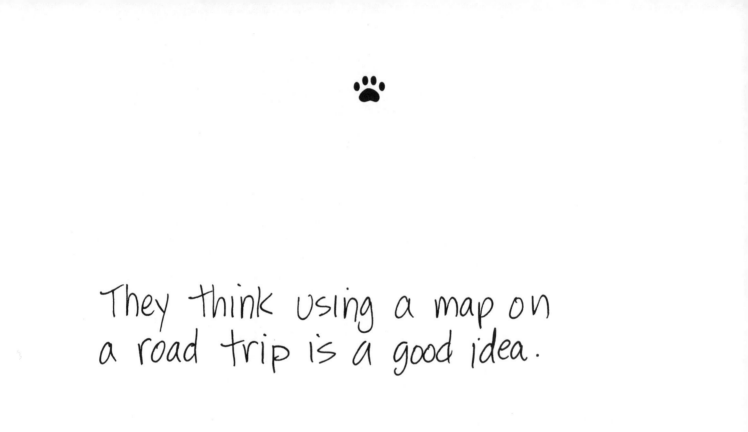

They think using a map on
a road trip is a good idea.

They're not too proud to ask
you for help when they need it.

And... they'd rather be with you than anyone else!!